Pursuing Awe

Celebrating Nature along the Mississippi River

By Capt. Larry Nielson

With contributions by Manda Hart Baldwin
and Janene Nelson

www.larrynielson.com

INTRODUCTION:

Modern life has no shortage of circumstances that contribute to stress, angst, anger, and fatigue. Mainstream news and social media are determined to make us angry. I don't want to be stressed out and angry! I often wonder how most of the negative news really affects my day to day life? The conclusion is that the vast majority of the negative news only affects us personally by sapping away our positive emotional and physical energy. It provides a negative view of the World and keeps us from noticing and appreciating all of the positive things surrounding us.

To preserve any semblance of sanity, other like-minded souls and myself have made it a daily habit to consciously seek out positive and awesome things each day. We spend some time appreciating those awesome things, often taking pictures so that we can share the positive experience with others.

Several years ago, my wife Nancy gave me a camera for Christmas and thus started a new hobby. A life-long Naturalist, I was able to explore the great outdoors and share all of the neat things I came across. I share many of those photos with friends who have subsequently encouraged me to put a collection of my thoughts and pictures into a book. This work is a result of that encouragement and is dedicated to all of you that provided the encouragement and to my wife Nancy who helped start me on this daily journey. Thanks to all of you that prompted, cajoled and encouraged me! I hope that this effort meets your expectations.

CONTENTS

The Humble Messenger

Standing at the edge of the woods, enveloped in the solitude of the pre-dawn darkness. Watching and listening, absorbed by my surroundings. An hour before dawn the birds shake themselves awake with a cacophony of songs, whistles and tweets. Coyotes yip in the distance and a turkey gobbles from somewhere deep in the woods. The pre-dawn sky is coming alive with a kaleidoscope of red, yellow, orange and blue reflecting on the wispy clouds and calm surface of the Lake. A pair of eagles chitter to each other across the valley to greet the coming day. About thirty minutes before dawn, the Sun's ambient light has already washed away the darkness. Squirrels, rabbits, and chipmunks scamper about in search of their morning meals. A sailboat is anchored on the Lake, surrounded in morning mist glowing in the twilight colors. Are the occupants sleeping or awake? Do they even realize the breathtaking scene that they are part of? A doe and two fawns cautiously step out of the woods, watch me, sense no danger, and expose themselves. The horizon explodes with the sun's warm rays. Dew glistens like jewels on the grass. Hummingbirds swarm the feeders. An eagle descends from the sky with talons out-stretched and grabs a fish for his breakfast. It all makes me feel small, humble and insignificant. A peaceful spirit rises in my chest, filling my soul with a deep sense of awe and energy. Deeply moved and awestruck by the experience, I need to share it with others through pictures and words. Not sure if my skills are adequate for the task, I am but a humble messenger.

Dawn's twilight 30 minutes before sunrise. Taken from our yard The pre-dawn is my favorite time of day!

No matter how many you have seen before, an eagle soaring above you is always a very cool thing to see!

A doe and fawn watching me in the early morning light

Hummingbird stretching his wings to greet the sunrise.
Taken from our deck in July.

My friends Angela and Karl Elser often
anchored their sailboat "Egress" across the
Lake from our house and they would spend the
night onboard. As the sun comes up and the
morning mist rises from Lake Pepin, they are
often enveloped in an awesome mystical scene
like this one on a September morning in 2015.
Karl and Angela are in the midst of a mission to
simplify their lives and make a daily habit of
appreciating Mother Nature's gifts. I would say
they are off to a great start in that direction.

EAGLES

Eagles are one of my favorite subjects. For the past few decades I have had the great fortune to live on the Mississippi River overlooking Lake Pepin, the largest Lake on the River. This area has an abundance of eagles. I see them almost every day as I go about my daily business and errands. We see an eagle's nest from our house and watch them add branches to the nest, guard their territory, fish, and care for their eaglets. It is impossible to watch eagles and not be filled with a sense of awe and appreciation. This chapter contains a few of my favorite eagle pictures.

February on the Mississippi River near Wabasha, MN

I saw this eagle watching the cars go by on Highway 61
between Wabasha and Lake City,MN on a day in
March

Eagles like to be on the ice. I have counted as many as 200
standing together on the edge of Lake Pepin's ice pack.

Taken from our yard. Several eagles were soaring
around in the wind currents that day.

Eagles are vociferous and make a "chittering" sound when they talk. Here is a good shot of one communicating

I saw this immature bald eagle on Highway 61 near my driveway. At this age they are very hard to distinguish between an immature bald and a Golden Eagle. The talons are a give away. Golden's have "hairy talons" with feathers covering their "ankles". Bald eagles are primarily fish eaters and the added weight of wet feathers near their talons would be an un-wanted extra burden.

From "Pearl of the Lake, October 2016.

Eating a fish at Reads Landing, MN

Snatching some dinner. At Reads Landing, MN

A humerous look of determination on this youngster as
he stalks towards a crow to take a fish away from it.

Don't even THINK about taking my fish away! At
Lake City, April 2014

From Highway 61 near Wabasha

A very unusual sight that I have only witnessed this one
time. I was watching this eagle from the helm of the
Pearl near Hok-si-la Park. It grabbed a large fish and
tried to fly away with it but the fish was to heavy to lift.
Not wanting to lose his prize, he held on tight with his
talons and swam to shore about 20 feet away. He
eventually dragged it out of the water and rested for
awhile before consumming his well deserved meal.

One of the great things about watching eagles in the winter is that you can get pretty close to them. The only way to tell the difference between male and female eagles is size. Females are generally larger and a couple of pounds heavier. Ths is a large female near the shore of Lake Pepin that I took in February, 2016.

A young bald eagle, at Colvill park in Red Wing

Life on the Mississippi River

I have always loved water. When very young, I would often spend the entire day playing in the creek that went through our backyard. When I was 10 years old we moved in to Rochester, MN about two blocks from the Zumbro River. I spent all of my free time fishing, hiking, wading and trapping muskrats and mink along the River bank. My sixteenth year was momentous, I could finally drive and purchased a car. My Grandparents also purchased a home that year on Lake Peterson, a backwater lake of the Mississippi River. I have many precious memories working alongside Grandpa as we added to and remodeled his home, cut and split firewood for the fireplace, fished and enjoyed the River. I saved enough money to buy my own boat and left it tied to his dock. Whenever I could, I would hop in my car and drive the 45 minutes to Grandpa's house, jump in the boat and head on out for a day of exploring the great River. Decades later I was finally able to build my own home on the Mississippi. There is always something cool to see and do on the River. This Chapter focuses on life along "Old Man River", its backwaters, and espcially its largest and most beautiful Lake, Lake Pepin.

The interstate bridge at Wabasha, MN just before dawn

November dawn on Lake Pepin

I was standing on the banks of the River watching the sunrise in August when the American Queen went by heading upstream. The morning sunlight reflecting off her stern made for a very awesome sight!

Dawn on the Mississippi River at Reads Landing, MN

For navigation purposes, the Mississippi River is actually two different Rivers, the Upper and Lower Mississippi with unique mile markers for each. The Lower Mississippi mile markers begin at the "Head of Passes", the point about 100 miles south of New Orleans where the River divides into three major forks that continue through the delta to the Gulf of Mexico. "Head of Passes" is zero and the mile markers upstream from that point are calculated as "Above Head of Passes" or AHP. They continue upstream to the confluence of the Ohio at 953 AHP. The Upper Mississippi Mile Markers begin at that same confluence and are termed Upper Mississippi River Miles (UMRM). Therefore, the confluence of the Ohio and Mississippi Rivers is labeled as both 953 AHP and 0 UMRM. The UMRM markers continue upstream 866 miles through the Twin Cities to the Coon Rapids Dam. During the Civil War the Union blockaded the Head of Passes which effectively kept any large draft vessels from leaving or entering the Mississippi River.

The River is about 2,500 miles long and is the fourth longest river in the world. Lake Itasca where the River starts is 1475 feet above sea level and of course it is at sea level where it empties into the Gulf of Mexico. Over half that drop in elevation, 800 feet, occurs in the State of Minnesota. A raindrop that falls on Lake Itasca takes about 90 days to reach the Gulf of Mexico.

October morning at Reads Landing, MN

Early October, from our deck

Misty sunrise on the River, at Reads Landing, MN

Fall colors at Maiden Rock Bluff on Lake Pepin

A Ring Billed Gull watching the sunrise at Lake City

Did this beaver take on more than he can chew? In the
Wisconsin backwaters

April sun brings out the turtles

A flock of Pelicans at Hastings, MN

I saw this unusual rainbow from our yard in May of
2015. Is it the stairway to heaven?

Stahli Park just north of Lake City. What a wonderful
spot to relax and read a book!

I took this picture in October. It is on the dike road between Wabasha, MN and Nelson, WI. This is a picture of the water reflecting the morning sunlight and trees.

Village of Pepin, WI reflecting on the Lake on a warm afternoon in late October. Doesn't it look idyllic?

November morning, just downstream from Lake Pepin.

A tow of empty barges heading upstream at Red Wing,
MN in late March. You can tell they are empty by how
far out of the water they are riding.

One barge holds the equivalent of 15 jumbo rail hoppers or 58 semi-truck trailers. A group of barges tied together is called a "tow". On the Upper River the average tow will contain 12 or 15 barges.

Barges below Maiden Rock Bluff, reflecting the sunset on a June Sunset Cruise onboard Pearl of the Lake

Upbound at Reads Landing, April 2013. The main channel is at least 9 feet deep to accommodate the barges. The 9 foot depth is maintained by using a system of locks and dams to regulate the river depth. There are 29 locks and dams on the Upper Mississippi and none on the lower Mississippi

Evening's twilight on the Wisconsin backwaters
December 2013

Rain squall on Lake Pepin, taken from the helm of
Pearl of the Lake, May 2016

My friend Manda Hart Baldwin is an exceptional photographer and an absolute expert at seeking out and capturing awesome sights every day! In the photo above she captured the Aurora Borealis(Northern Lights) over Lake Pepin. In the photo below, she did an extraordinary job capturing a December sunrise coming up over Lake Pepin. She is certainly a very gifted and inspiring talent!

Great River Heartbeat

Standing on the banks of the Great River
the current rolls on and on and on,
alive and pulsing, pulsing, pulsing.
The lifeblood of Mother Earth.

Muskrats slide down the bank
disappearing below the surface.
A beaver pulls a branch upstream
adding to his family's home.

Fish boil the water's smooth surface
the eagle's keen eye spy's them for breakfast.
An osprey circles from high above
water exploding when as he dives for his meal.

The ducks and the swans and the geese
are swimming and feeding together in a group.
Gulls furiously tumbling and circling
as they grab insects from the sky.

The sun and the clouds and the trees
reflect idyllic on the smooth surface.
Ripples gently lap the shore by my feet,
the peaceful whisper of the Great River's heartbeat.

And the current rolls on and on and on,
Taking with it some of my heart and soul.
Together now , we are pulsing, pulsing, pulsing.
The lifeblood of Mother Earth.

Larry Nielson

Pearl of the Lake Riverboat

In the summer between 5th and 6th grade I ordered a kit to build a canvas canoe. I possessed the carpentry skills of any average 11 year old and when completed my Mother was dubious that it would even float. But float it did, providing many hours of enjoyment before it finally broke apart a few months later. Over the subsequent years I would own many other pleasure boats of almost every type made. Eventually in 2005 I purchased a 129 passenger paddlewheel boat. She was built in 1982 in LaCrosse, WI, spent her first few years working in Winona, MN as the "Winona Princess". From 1988 – 2001 she was in Clarksville, TN and was known as the "Queen of Clarksville". In 2003 and 2004 she operated out of Fort Smith, Arkansas as the "Arkansas River Queen". By 2004 her hull had developed electrolysis, rusted full of pin holes, and was condemned to dry-dock at a boat yard in North Little Rock. We purchased her in 2006, cut the rusted hull off and renovated her into "ship shape" condition. We brought her home to Lake City and re-christened her "Pearl of the Lake" where she has been providing cruises on Lake Pepin ever since.

Pearl of the Lake off Marina Point

Pearl of the Lake passengers enjoying a beautiful
morning on Lake Pepin

Just before a sunrise coffee cruise in October 2016

Back to the dock after an evening cruise

Fall color cruise, November 1, 2013

"Super Moon" over Lake Pepin on a sunset cruise in
July 2014

Pearl is the perfect venue for a romantic wedding and
we help many couples start their married lives together
each year.

One of my favorite pictures, I took this on a sunset cruise when we were near "Point No Point" while the sunset lined up with the flag on our stern.

May 2013,a beautiful Spring day while we were getting ready for the upcoming season.

Full moon on a sunset cruise in July, 2015

Sunset Cruise in October 2016

Sunset through Pearl's rigging

July Sunset Cruise on Pearl of the Lake

Sunrises and Sunsets

Although the Mississippi River runs primarily North to South, in our area it twist and runs from West to East, which makes for stunning sunrises and sunsets. The sunrises are my personal favorite because by nature I am early riser and look forward to the opportunities of a coming day. The early morning solitude and watching the World come alive excites me. In the summer months the sun comes up right across the Lake from our house, so I often get up before dawn, make a pot of coffee, grab my camera, and watch the dawn from the park bench in our yard.

Sunsets are also cool, primarily because more often than not I am with other people sharing the experience. Many of those sunsets are onboard the Pearl and often the experience is so cool that the passengers and crew develop a special bond from having witnessed it together. This chapter shows a few of my favorite sunrises on sunsets.

The beach in Pepin, WI at Sunset

October Sunrise at the Interstate Bridge in Wabasha

Sunrise in March from Marina Point in Lake City.

July sunset from Pearl of the Lake, Central Point in the foreground, Hok-Si-La Park in the background.

April sunrise bursting over Lake Pepin, from our yard.

May Sunrise, from our deck

August sunset from Pearl of the Lake

July sunrise from our woods.

Hummingbird at dawn in our yard

September sunset over Lake Pepin. Taken on Highway
61 between Lake City and Wabasha

Morning mist rising from the Wisconsin hills just
downstream from Pepin, WI. Taken at dawn from the
Minnesota side of the river on Highway 61 in August.

October dawn at Reads Landing, MN

August dawn at Lake City.

August sunrise on Lake Pepin, alongside Highway 61
between Lake City and Wabasha.

Dawn on November 15, 2013 from our deck

A stroll in the woods

The mid-summer afternoon sun is hot on my bare back. I step into the woods and the air is perceptively cooler. The tree canopy offers shade, but there is also a cool breath of air emanating from the woods. Standing still, absorbing the breeze and wondering where it comes from? It seems to come from everywhere, as if the woods are alive, a breathing creature. I wonder exactly how much cooler it is inside the forest? I resolve to someday bring a thermometer and find out. Slowly walking up the old logging trail, recognizing and saying hello to my old tree friends. Many of them were seedlings long before I was born and others will still be here long after my departure. The leafs are picturesque against the bright blue sky. My eyes follow their branches to the trunks, and then the trunks down to the forest floor. Each tree is an individual. Some branches and trunks are nearly straight while others twist and turn in gnarled confusion. Some start out as one large trunk and seem to split into two trees. A few start out as two nearby trunks that grow together and form one tree as it stretches to the sky. Some are scorched and disfigured from lightning strikes and still others have burls growing on them. I wonder what forces of nature or fate caused the abnormalities? I conclude that the unique ones are much more identifiable and interesting than the perfect ones. Why dot we often cull them in an absurd quest for perfection? I ruminate that maybe it is the same way we treat people,,,, and how much do we lose as a result? Some of the trees are very old, some are middle age, and others are just a one leaf twig sprouting from the ground. Together the individuals form a family, a living breathing familial society that we call a woods or forest.

I sit down on the forest floor, silently absorbing the surroundings, watching the birds and the squirrels and the chipmunks. Staying very still to see how close they will come to me. A curious chipmunk scampers nearby, three feet away from me, then two. We lock eyes and I wonder if he is brave enough to come and sit in my lap? He is not, and scampers away. I notice an amazing variety of plants. In particular, the ferns, wildflowers and mushrooms catch my eye. I reach out my hand and sweep away some decaying leafs to see what lies below. A few exposed earthworms twist into the soft ground. I find some snails, beetles and other bugs that I don't recognize. About one hundred feet away a group of three turkeys peck at acorns beneath an old oak tree. Up the slope in the other direction is a small patch that was burned off by a wildfire. The trees burned away and now are replaced by a thick assortment of sumac and various tree saplings about ten feet high. I know that deer often bed down in that thicket and watch as a doe eats leafs off a tender sapling. It is interesting that the old oak and the young sapling both support life in their own special way. A look at my watch reveals that I have been in the woods for a few hours now and my everyday duties are calling. I stand up and stretch my aging muscles before heading back down the trail. A few hours in the woods have cleared my cluttered mind and brought some clarity to everyday issues. I ponder on how this family of trees provides protection, sustenance and peace for many plants and creatures both great and small, including me. With a debt of gratitude, I owe it to them to return the favor as best I can.

Our woods drenched by the dawn's soft glow

Sunrise reflecting on the forest floor and a rotting tree
stump

I call this one our Butt tree because it looks like a
human butt. It is actually two trees that grew together.

The Path in our woods

It is always a welcoming site to pull off the highway
and onto our driveway

A buck watching me in the yard.

Wildflowers growing at the edge of our woods.

Interesting mushroom growing on a tree in our woods.

I came upon this mushroom on a walk in our woods in
early November and thought it was cool.

I often sit and watch hummingbirds for hours at a time. They are fascinating and unique, with abilities that no other creature on earth possesses. The joint where their wings are attached to the body is much like a human wrist, able to move in almost any direction. This gives them the ability to hover in space or fly in any direction, including backwards. They eat insects and nectar, in the Spring following the blooming flowers north from Central America to our area and even further north. They don't really "suck" nectar, they scoop it in with a forked tongue that extends and contracts up to 20 times per second. Their respiratory system is so efficient they virtually never get winded and can thrive in atmospheres with only 7% oxygen (higher than the tallest mountains or what a modern airliner can cruise at). Experts say that there are over 300 species of hummingbirds in the World, all of them in the Americas. 17 of those species live in North America, the Ruby Throated being the species we see in our area. They normally arrive in May and leave by Mid-September. Watching hummers is truly an awesome experience!

Hummingbirds at the feeder that hangs in our Living Room window.

In the wild, hummers tend to be territorial. In a yard with plenty of feeders they are social and we often see as many as twenty of them feeding together.

White hummingbirds are very rare with less than 200
sightings ever reported. We saw this one hanging out
around our house for about eight weeks in the summer
of 2012. Albinos have pink eyes, peak and feet. This
one is called "Leucistic", which means that they are
white but have some coloration and are not true albino.
It was a real treat to witness this rare bird and our
pictures of him were published in several magazines
and nature web sites.

My friends Janene and Mitch Nelson farm near Pepin, WI. Janene is an expert at searching out and capturing awesome things that most of us over look. She has a great eye for detail and inspires me to look closely at every-day things.

Janene Nelson has the special gift to turn the
simplest things into great art!

Winter Wonders

This book is all about finding and appreciating the awesome things around us every day. It would be in-complete if it didn't include a chapter about all the great winter scenes that Nature provides. If you approach a winter day searching for something awesome to see you will almost never be disappointed!

March sunrise over Lake Pepin, taken from Lake City
at the end of Marina Point

The Interstate bridge at Wabasha on a January morning

A pressure ridge on Lake Pepin in January. As the Lake
makes ice, and if there is not much snow on it to muffle
sound, the Lake ice will "sing", moan, groan & thunder
as it pops under the pressure of the ice pack growing.

Taking the dogs for a walk in our woods in February

Frosty leaf by Janene Nelson

A February morning in our back yard

Lake Pepin in January

Iconic Americana one room school house south of
Rochester,MN. Despite its poor condition it still holds
many happy memories for me because I attended this
school for the first four years of my formal education.
First through Sixth grade, there were 16 of us attending
with three kids in my grade. The largest class was the
one ahead of me, it had four girls in it. We drew our
drinking water from the hand pump out front. During
inclement weather the teacher would read us chapters
from "Little House on the Prairie" books.

It is somewhat ironic that I now can look out our living
room window across the Lake and see Pepin, WI
which was the birthplace of Laura Ingalls Wilder and
the subject of her first book, "Little House in the Big
Woods".

The storefronts in Lake City lit up by the morning
sunrise on a March morning

January Sunrise on Lake Pepin, taken from Lake City

A small creek south of Lake City

Rush River near Maiden Rock, WI in January

A flock of tundra swans with the dawn sunlight reflecting on them. December at Reads Landing

Tundra swans at dawn, December 2016

Soothing the Soul

My friend Rebecca Paquette Johnson owns BNOX
Gold and Iron in Pepin, WI. Her studio overlooks Lake
Pepin and she definitely appreciates it. She once told
me that Lake Pepin "soothes your soul" . I have to
agree with her. We all need a little soul soothing at
times. This chapter attempts to do just that.

Sunrise from our deck

Lake Pepin, from Pearl of the Lake in June 2016

Lake Pepin looking downstream from Lake City in
September

August sunrise from the Lake City Sportsman's Club

March 31 on Lake Pepin

Misty morning sunrise, from Highway 61.

March Sunrise from our deck, notice the ice pack is still
on the Lake in the left side of this photo.

Sunday afternoon in July, from our deck

September sunset from Pearl of the Lake

October reflections on Lake Pepin

Sailboats below Maiden Rock Bluff

A lazy summer afternoon relaxing on the Lake

Sunset near Point No Point

Lake Pepin Facts

Lake Pepin is a natural lake created thousands of years ago by the natural topography of the area. Almost all other lakes on the river are actually man made reservoirs created by a dam. It is also the largest lake on the entire River, 22 miles long by 2 miles wide, an average depth of about 25 feet with the deepest spot about 85 feet deep.

Lake Pepin is almost identical in size and topography to another World famous Lake, Loch Ness in Scotland. Like Loch Ness, Lake Pepin has a mysterious creature swimming in its depths known as the lake monster "Pepie". Pepie has been sighted many times over the past several hundred years and is part of the local Native American folklore.

World famous author Laura Ingalls Wilder was born near Pepin,WI and every year thousands of people come to see the replica cabin built on the original site of the Ingalls farm.

Waterskiing was invented on Lake Pepin in 1922 by Lake City native Ralph Samuelson.

Lake Pepin freezes solid in the winter with 2-3 feet of ice because even though the Mississippi River runs all of the way through Lake Pepin, there is no discernible current on the Lake. Above and below the Lake, the river current is normally moving along at around 5 miles per hour but when it reaches the Lake the water spreads out and the current dissipates.

Do not endeavor to change others. It is a tremendous task just to change yourself and it is impossible to change others. The best that you can hope for is to influence them with your positive attitude, ethics, kindness and actions.

Larry Nielson